The Articles of the State Constitutions:
An Index Guide

New England (Region 1): Connecticut, Maine, Massachusetts,
New Hampshire, Rhode Island, and Vermont

Bootblack Budget Books
Copyright 2018 ©
ISBN-13: 978-1727179361
ISBN-10: 1727179366

Table of Contents To This Book:

The Constitution of The State of Connecticut – Page 3

The Constitution of The State of Maine – Page 4

The Constitution of The State of Massachusetts – Page 23

The Constitution of The State of New Hampshire – Page 29

The Constitution of The State of Rhode Island – Page 40

The Constitution of The State of Vermont – Page 58

The Constitution of The State of Connecticut

Preamble — Page 03

Article I: Declaration of Rights – Page 04

Article II: Of the Distribution of Powers – Page 08

Article III: Of the Legislative Department – Page 09

Article IV: Of the Executive Department – Page 16

Article V: Of the Judicial Department – Page 24

Article VI: Of the Qualifications of the Electors – Page 26

Article VII: Of Religion – Page 29

Article VIII: Of Education – Page 30

Article XIX: Of Impeachments – Page 31

Article X: Of Home Rule – Page 32

Article XI: General Provisions – Page 33

Article XII: Of Amendments to the Constitution – Page 35

Article XIII: Of Constitutional Conventions – Page 36

Article XIV: The Effective Date of this Constitution — Page 38

The Constitution of The State of Maine

Preamble – Page 22

Article I: Declaration of Rights – Page 23

Section 1. Natural Rights

Section 2. Power Inherent in People

Section 3. Religious Freedom; Sects Equal; Religious Tests Prohibited; Religious Teachers

Section 4. Freedom of Speech and Publication; Libel; Truth Given in Evidence; Jury Determines Law and Fact

Section 5. Unreasonable Searches Prohibited

Section 6. Rights of Persons Accused

Section 6-A. Discrimination Against Persons Prohibited

Section 7. No Person to Answer to Certain Crimes But on Indictment; Exceptions; Juries

Section 8. No Double Jeopardy

Section 9. Sanguinary Laws, Excessive Bail, Cruel or Unusual Punishments Prohibited

Section 10. Bailable Offenses; Habeas Corpus

Section 11. Attainder, Ex Post Facto And Contract-Impairment Laws Prohibited

Section 12. Treason; Testimony of 2 Witnesses

Section 13. Suspension of Laws

Section 14. Corporal Punishment Under Military Law

Section 15. Right of Petition

Section 16. To Keep and Bear Arms

Section 17. Standing Armies

Section 18. Quartering of Soldiers on Citizens

Section 19. Right of Redress for Injuries

Section 20. Trial by Jury

Section 21. Private Property, When to be Taken

Section 22. Taxes

Section 23. Title of Nobility Prohibited; Tenure of Offices

Section 24. Other Rights not Impaired

Article II: Electors – Page 29

Section 1. Qualifications of Electors; Written Ballot; Military Servicemen; Students

Section 2. Electors Exempt from Arrests on Election Days

Section 3. Exemption from Military Duty

Section 4. Time of State Election; Absentee Voting

Section 5. Voting Machines

Article III: Distribution of Powers – Page 31

Section 1. Powers Distributed

Section 2. To be Kept Separate

Article IV: Part First - House of Representatives – Page 32

Section 1. Legislative Department; Style of Acts

Section 2. Number of Representatives; Biennial Terms; Division of the State into Districts for House of Representatives

Section 3. Submission of Reapportionment Plan to Clerk of House; Legislature's Action on Commission's Plan

Section 4. Qualifications; Residency Requirement

Section 5. Election of Representatives; Lists of Votes Delivered Forthwith; Lists of Votes Examined By Governor; Summons of Persons Who Appear to be Elected; Lists Shall be Laid Before the House

Section 6. Vacancies

Section 7. To Choose Own Officers

Section 8. Power of Impeachment

Article IV: Part Second – Senate – Page 36

Section 1. Number of Senators

Section 2. Submission of Reapportionment Plan to Secretary of Senate; Legislature's Action on Commission's Plan; Division of State into Senatorial Districts; Division by Supreme Judicial Court.

Section 3. Election of Senators; Lists of Votes Delivered Forthwith

Section 4. Lists of Votes Examined by Governor; Summons to Persons Who Appear to be Elected

Section 5. Determination of Senators Elected; Procedure for Filling Vacancies

Section 6. Qualifications

Section 7. To Try Impeachments; Limitation of Judgment of Impeachment; Party Liable to be Tried and Punished in Court

Section 8. To Choose Own Officers

Article IV: Part Third - Legislative Power – Page 39

Section 1. To Meet Annually; Power of Legislature to Convene Itself at Other Times; Extent of Legislative Power

Section 1-A. Legislature to Establish Apportionment Commission; Number of Quorum; Compensation of Commission Members; Commission's Budget; Division Among Political Parties

Section 2. Bills to be Signed by the Governor; Proceedings, in Case the Governor Disapproves; Allowing the Governor 10 Days to Act on Legislation

Section 2-A. Line-Item Veto Of Dollar Amounts Appearing in Appropriation or Allocation Sections of Legislative Documents

Section 3. Each House the Judge of its Elections; Majority, A Quorum

Section 4. May Punish and Expel Members

Section 5. Shall Keep a Journal; Yeas and Nays

Section 6. May Punish for Contempt

Section 7. Compensation; Traveling Expenses

Section 8. Members Exempt From Arrest; Freedom of Debate

Section 9. Either House May Originate Bills; Revenue Bills

Section 10. Members not to be Appointed to Certain Offices

Section 11. Persons Disqualified to be Members

Section 12. Adjournments

Section 13. Special Legislation

Section 14. Corporations, Formed Under General Laws

Section 15. Constitutional Conventions

Section 16. Acts Become Effective in 90 Days After Recess; Exception; Emergency Bill Defined

Section 17. Proceedings for People's Veto

1. Petition Procedure; Petition for People's Veto
2. Effect of Referendum
3. Referral to Electors; Proclamation by Governor

Section 18. Direct Initiative of Legislation

1. Petition Procedure
2. Referral to Electors Unless Enacted by the Legislature Without Change; Number of Signatures Necessary on Direct Initiative Petitions; Dating Signatures on Petitions; Competing Measures
3. Timing of Elections; Proclamation by Governor

Section 19. Effective Date of Measures Approved by People; Veto Power Limited.

Section 20. Meaning of Words "Electors," "People," "Recess of Legislature," "Statewide Election," "Measure," "Circulator," and "Written Petition"; Written Petitions for People's Veto; Written Petitions for Direct Initiative

Section 21. City Council of Any City May Establish Direct Initiative and People's Veto

Section 22. Election Officers and Officials, How Governed

Section 23. Municipalities Reimbursed Annually

Article V: Part First - Executive Power – Page 54

Section 1. Governor

Section 2. Term of Office; Reelection Eligibility

Section 3. Election; Votes to be Returned to Secretary of State; Secretary of State to Lay Lists Before the Senate and House of Representatives; Provision in Case of Tie

Section 4. Qualifications

Section 5. Disqualifications

Section 6. Compensation

Section 7. Commander in Chief

Section 8. To Appoint Officers

Section 9. To Give Information and Recommend Measures

Section 10. May Require Information of any Officer

Section 11. Power to Pardon and Remit Penalties, Etc.; Conditions

Section 12. Shall Enforce the Laws

Section 13. Convene the Legislature on Extraordinary Occasions, and Adjourn it in Case of Disagreement; May Change the Place of Meeting

Section 14. Vacancy, How Supplied

Section 15. Temporary Mental or Physical Disability of Governor

Article V: Part Second – Secretary – Page 61

Section 1. Election

Section 1-A. Succession to the Office of Secretary of State

Section 2. Records of State; Deputies.

Section 3. Attend the Governor, Senate, and House

Article V: Part Third -Treasurer – Page 62

Section 1. Election

Section 1-A. Succession to the Office of Treasurer

Section 2. Bond

Section 3. Not to Engage in Trade

Section 4. No Money Drawn Except Upon Appropriation or Allocation

Section 5. Bonding Regulations; Prohibiting use of Proceeds From Sale of Bonds to Fund Current Expenditures

Article VI: Judicial Power – Page 64

Section 1. Courts

Section 2. Compensation

Section 3. To Give Opinion When Required by Governor or Either Branch of the Legislature

Section 4. Tenure of Judicial Officers; 6-Month Holdover Period

Section 5. Limitation on Holding Other Office

Section 6. Judges and Registers of Probate, Election and Tenure; Vacancies

Article VII: Military – Page 66

Section 1. Officers, How Appointed

Section 2. Qualifications and Selection

Section 3. Adjutant General

Section 4. Standard of Organization, Armament and Discipline

Section 5. Persons Exempt From Military Duty

Article VIII: Part First – Education – Page 68

Section 1. Legislature Shall Require Towns to Support Public Schools; Duty of Legislature

Section 2. Authority to Pledge the Credit of the State and to Issue Bonds for Loans to Maine Students in Higher Education and Their Parents

Article VIII: Part Second - Municipal Home Rule – Page 69

Section 1. Power of Municipalities to Amend Their Charters

Section 2. Construction of Buildings for Industrial Use

Article IX: General Provisions – Page 70

Section 1. Oaths and Subscriptions

Section 2. Offices Incompatible With Each Other; Election to Congress Disqualifies

Section 3. Commissions

Section 4. Elections on the First Wednesday After First Tuesday of January may be Adjourned From Day to Day

Section 5. Removal by Impeachment or Address

Section 6. Tenure of Office

Section 7. Valuation

Section 8. Taxation

1. Intangible Property
2. Assessment of Certain Lands Based on Current Use; Penalty on Change to Higher Use
3. School Districts
4. Watercraft
5. Historic and Scenic Preservation

Section 9. Power of Taxation

Section 10. Tenure of Sheriffs, Removal of Sheriffs from Office and Replacement

Section 11. Attorney General

Section 12. Voting Districts

Section 13. Bribery at elections

Section 14. Authority and Procedure for Issuance of Bonds

Section 14-A. Authority to Insure Industrial, Manufacturing, Fishing, and Agricultural Mortgage Loans

Section 14-B. Authority to Insure Revenue Bonds of the Maine School Building Authority

Section 14-C. Authority to Insure Mortgage Loans for Indian Housing

Section 14-D. Authority to Insure Maine Veterans Mortgage Loans, and to Appropriate Moneys And Issue Bonds for the Payment of Same

Section 15. Municipal Borrowing Regulated by Legislature Through General Law

Section 16. Seat of Government

Section 17. Continuity of Government in Case of Enemy Attack

Section 18. Limitation on Use of Funds of Maine State Retirement System

Section 18-A. Funding of Retirement Benefits Under the Maine State Retirement System

Section 18-B. Payment of Unfunded Liabilities of the Maine State Retirement System

Section 19. Limitation on Expenditure of Motor Vehicle and Motor Vehicle Fuel Revenues

Section 20. Mining Excise Tax Trust Fund

Section 21. State Mandates

Section 22. Revenues Generated by Fisheries and Wildlife Management

Section 23. State Park Land

Section 24. Reapportionment

1. Procedure
2. Court Apportionment
3. Judicial Review

Section 25. Apportionment of County Commissioner Districts

1. Redistricting, Generally
2. Supreme Judicial Court

Article X: Additional Provisions – Page 87

Section 1. (See Section 7 Note)

Section 2. (See Section 7 And Note)

Section 3. Laws Now in Force Continue Until Repealed

Section 4. Amendments to Constitution

Section 5. (See Section 7 And Note)

Section 6. Constitution to be Arranged by Chief Justice of the Supreme Judicial Court; Constitution to be Enrolled and Printed With Laws; Supreme Law of the State

Section 7. Original Sections 1, 2, 5, of Article X not to be Printed; Section 5 in Full Force

The Constitution of The State of Massachusetts

Preamble

Part The First: A Declaration of the Rights of the Inhabitants of the Commonwealth of Massachusetts

Article I – Page 9
Article II – Page 10
Article III – Page 11
Article IV – Page 13
Article V – Page 14
Article VI – Page 15
Article VII – Page 16
Article VIII – Page 17
Article IX – Page 18
Article X – Page 19
Article XI – Page 20
Article XII – Page 21
Article XIII – Page 22
Article XIV – Page 23
Article XV – Page 24
Article XVI – Page 25
Article XVII – Page 26
Article XVIII – Page 27
Article XIX – Page 28
Article XX – Page 29
Article XXI – Page 30
Article XXII – Page 31
Article XXIII – Page 32
Article XXIV – Page 33
Article XXV – Page 34
Article XXVI – Page 35
Article XXVII – Page 36
Article XXVIII – Page 37
Article XXIX – Page 38
Article XXX – Page 39

Part The Second: The Frame of Government

Frame of Government – Page 40

Chapter I: The Legislative Power

Section I. The General Court:

Article I – Page 41
Article II – Page 42
Article III – Page 43
Article IV – Page 44

Section II. The Senate:

Article I – Page 47
Article II – Page 48
Article III– Page 50
Article IV– Page 51
Article V – Page 52
Article VI– Page 53
Article VII– Page 54
Article VIII– Page 55
Article IX – Page 56

Section III. House of Representatives:

Article I – Page 57
Article II – Page 58
Article III– Page 59
Article IV– Page 60
Article V – Page 61
Article VI– Page 62
Article VII– Page 63
Article VIII– Page 64
Article IX – Page 65
Article X – Page 66
Article XI – Page 67

Chapter II: Executive Power

Section I. The Governor:

Article I – Page 68
Article II – Page 69
Article III– Page 70
Article IV– Page 71
Article V – Page 72
Article VI– Page 73
Article VII– Page 74
Article VIII– Page 76

Article IX – Page 77
Article X – Page 78
Article XI – Page 80
Article XII – Page 81
Article XIII – Page 82

Section II. Lieutenant-Governor:

Article I – Page 83
Article II – Page 84
Article III – Page 85

Section III. Council, and the Manner of Settling Elections by the Legislature:

Article I – Page 86
Article II – Page 87
Article III – Page 88
Article IV – Page 89
Article V – Page 90
Article VI – Page 91
Article VII – Page 92

Section IV: Secretary, Treasurer, Commissary, Etc:

Article I – Page 93
Article II – Page 94

Chapter III: Judiciary Power:

Article I – Page 95
Article II – Page 96
Article III – Page 97
Article IV – Page 99
Article V – Page 100

Chapter IV: Delegates to Congress – Page 100

Chapter V: The University at Cambridge, and Encouragement of Literature, Etc:

Section I. The University

Article I – Page 101
Article II – Page 102
Article III – Page 103

Section II. The Encouragement of Literature, Etc. – Page 104

Chapter VI: Oaths and Subscriptions; Incompatibility of and Exclusion from Offices; Pecuniary Qualifications; Commissions; Writs; Confirmation of Laws; Habeas Corpus; The Enacting Style; Continuance of Officers; Provision for a Future Revisal of the Constitution, Etc.

Article I – Page 105
Article II – Page 108
Article III– Page 110
Article IV– Page 111
Article V – Page 112
Article VI– Page 113
Article VII– Page 114
Article VIII– Page 115
Article IX – Page 116
Article X – Page 117
Article XI – Page 118

ARTICLES OF AMENDMENT:

Article I – Page 119
Article II – Page 120
Article III – Page 121
Article IV – Page 122
Article V – Page 123
Article VI – Page 124
Article VII – Page 125
Article VIII – Page 126
Article IX – Page 127
Article X – Page 128
Article XI – Page 130
Article XII – Page 131
Article XIII – Page 133
Article XIV – Page 136
Article XV – Page 137
Article XVI – Page 138
Article XVII – Page 140
Article XVIII – Page 141
Article XIX – Page 142
Article XX – Page 143
Article XXI – Page 144
Article XXII – Page 146
Article XXIII – Page 147
A**rticle XXIV** – Page 148
Article XXV – Page 149
Article XXVI – Page 150
Article XXVII – Page 151
Article XXVIII – Page 152
Article XXIX – Page 153
Article XXX – Page 154
Article XXXI – Page 155
Article XXXII – Page 156
Article XXXIII – Page 157
Article XXXIV – Page 158
Article XXXV – Page 159
Article XXXVI – Page 160
Article XXXVII – Page 161
Article XXXVIII – Page 162
Article XXXIX – Page 163
Article XL – Page 164
Article XLI – Page 165
Article XLII – Page 166
Article XLIII – Page 167
Article XLIV – Page 168
Article XLV – Page 169
Article XLVI – Page 170
Article XVIII – Page 171
Article XLVII – Page 173
Article XLVIII – Page 174
Article XLIX – Page 189
Article L – Page 190
Article LI – Page 191
Article LII – Page 192
Article LIII – Page 193
Article LIV – Page 194
Article LV – Page 195
Article LVI – Page 196
Article LVII – Page 197
Article LVIII – Page 198
Article LIX – Page 199
Article LX – Page 200
Article LXI – Page 201
Article LXII – Page 202
Article LXIII – Page 203
Article LXIV – Page 205
Article LXV – Page 206
Article LXVI – Page 207
Article LXVII – Page 208
Article LXVIII – Page 209
Article LXIX – Page 210
Article LXX – Page 211
Article LXXI – Page 212

Article LXXII – Page 215
Article LXXIII – Page 216
Article LXXIV – Page 217
Article LXXV – Page 220
Article LXXVI – Page 221
Article LXXVII – Page 222
Article LXXVIII – Page 223
Article LXXIX – Page 224
Article LXXX – Page 225
Article LXXXII – Page 231
Article LXXXIII – Page 233
Article LXXXIV – Page 234
Article LXXXV – Page 235
Article LXXXVI – Page 236
Article LXXXVII – Page 237
Article LXXXVIII – Page 239
Article LXXXIX – Page 240
Article XC – Page 246
Article XCI – Page 248
Article XCII – Page 250
Article XCIII – Page 252
Article XCIV – Page 253
Article XCV – Page 254
Article XCVI – Page 255
Article XCVII – Page 256
Article XCVIII – Page 257
Article XCIX – Page 258
Article C – Page 259
Article CI – Page 260
Article CII – Page 262
Article CIII – Page 263
Article CIV – Page 264
Article CV – Page 265
Article CVI – Page 266
Article CVII – Page 267
Article CVIII – Page 268
Article CIX – Page 269
Article CX – Page 270
Article CXI – Page 271
Article CXII – Page 272
Article CXIII – Page 273
Article CXIV – Page 274
Article CXV – Page 275
Article CXVI – Page 276
Article CXVII – Page 277
Article CXVIII – Page 278
Article CXIX – Page 279
Article CXX – Page 280

The Constitution of
The State of New Hampshire

PART FIRST- BILL OF RIGHTS – Page 13

Article 1. Equality of Men; Origin and Object of Government

Article 2. Natural Rights

Article 2-A. The Bearing of Arms

Article 3. Society, it's Organization and Purposes

Article 4. Rights of Conscience Unalienable

Article 5. Religious Freedom Recognized

Article 6. Morality and Piety

Article 7. State Sovereignty

Article 8. Accountability of Magistrates and Officers; Public's Right to Know

Article 9. No Hereditary Office Or Place

Article 10. Right of Revolution

Article 11. Elections and Elective Franchises

Article 12. Protection and Taxation Reciprocal

Article 12-A. Power To Take Property Limited

Article 13. Conscientious Objectors not Compelled to Bear Arms

Article 14. Legal Remedies to be Free, Complete, and Prompt

Article 15. Right of Accused

Article 16. Former Jeopardy; Jury Trial in Capital Cases

Article 17. Venue of Criminal Prosecution

Article 18. Penalties to be Proportioned to Offenses; True Design of Punishment

Article 19. Searches and Seizures Regulated

Article 20. Jury Trial in Civil Causes

Article 21. Jurors; Compensation

Article 22. Free Speech; Liberty of The Press

Article 23. Retrospective Laws Prohibited

Article 24. Militia

Article 25. Standing Armies

Article 26. Military, Subject to Civil Power

Article 27. Quartering of Soldiers

Article 28. Taxes, by Whom Levied

Article 28-A. Mandated Programs

Article 29. Suspension of Laws by Legislature Only

Article 30. Freedom of Speech

Article 31. Meetings of Legislature, For What Purposes

Article 32. Rights of Assembly, Instruction, and Petition

Article 33. Excessive Bail, Fines, and Punishments Prohibited

Article 34. Martial Law Limited

Article 35. The Judiciary; Tenure of Office, Etc

Article 36. Pensions

Article 36-A. Use of Retirement Funds

Article 37. Separation of Powers

Article 38. Social Virtues Inculcated

Article 39. Changes in Town and City Charters; Referendum Required

PART SECOND --- FORM OF GOVERNMENT

Name of Body Politic – Page 25

Article 1. Name of Body Politic

General Court – Page 26

Article 2. Legislature, How Constituted

Article 3. General Court, When to Meet and Dissolve

Article 4. Power of General Court to Establish Courts

Article 5. Power to Make Laws, Elect Officers, Define Their Powers and Duties, Impose Fines, and Assess Taxes; Prohibited From Authorizing Towns to Aid Certain Corporations

Article 5-A. Continuity of Government in Case of Enemy Attack

Article 5-B. Power to Provide For Tax Valuations Based On Use

Article 6. Valuation and Taxation

Article 6-A. Use of Certain Revenues Restricted to Highways

Article 6-B. Use of Lottery Revenues Restricted to Educational Purposes

Article 7. Members of Legislature not to Take Fees Or Act As Counsel

Article 8. Open Sessions of Legislature

HOUSE OF REPRESENTATIVES – Page 31

Article 9. Representatives Elected Every Second Year; Apportionment of Representatives

Article 9-A. Legislative Adjustments of Census With Reference to Non-Residents

Article 10. Repealed

Article 11. Small Towns, Representation by Districts and Floterial Districts

Article 11-A. Division of Town, Ward, Or Place; Representative Districts

Article 12. Biennial Election of Representatives in November

Article 13. Repealed

Article 14. Representatives, How Elected, Qualifications of

Article 15. Compensation of The Legislature

Article 16. Vacancies in House, How Filled

Article 17. House to Impeach Before The Senate

Article 18. Money Bills to Originate in House

Article 18-A. Budget Bills

Article 19. Adjournment

Article 20. Quorum, What Constitutes

Article 21. Privileges of Members of The Legislature

Article 22. House to Elect Speaker and Officers, Settle Rules of Proceedings, and Punish Misconduct

Article 23. Senate and Executive Have Like Powers; Imprisonment Limited

Article 24. Journals and Laws to be Published; Yeas and Nays, and Protests

SENATE – Page 37

Article 25. Senate; How Constituted

Article 26. Senatorial Districts, How Constituted

Article 26-A. Division of Town, Ward, Or Lace; Senatorial Districts

Article 27. Election of Senators

Article 28. Repealed

Article 29. Qualifications of Senators

Article 30. Inhabitant Defined

Article 31. Inhabitants of Unincorporated Places; Their Rights, Etc

Article 32. Biennial Meetings, How Warned, Governed, and Conducted; Return of Votes, Etc

Article 33. Secretary of State to Count Votes For Senators and Notify Persons Elected

Article 34. Vacancies in Senate, How Filled

Article 35. Senate, Judges of Their Own Elections

Article 36. Adjournment

Article 37. Senate to Elect Their Own Officers; Quorum

Article 38. Senate to Try Impeachments; Mode of Proceeding

Article 39. Judgment On Impeachment Limited

Article 40. Chief Justice to Preside On Impeachment of Governor

EXECUTIVE POWER – GOVERNOR – Page 42

Article 41. Governor, Supreme Executive Magistrate

Article 42. Election of Governor, Return of Votes; Electors; If No Choice, Legislature to Elect One of Two Highest Candidates; Qualifications For Governor

Article 43. in Cases of Disagreement, Governor to Adjourn or Prorogue Legislature; If Causes Exist, May Convene Them Elsewhere

Article 44. Veto to Bills

Article 45. Resolves to be Treated Like Bills

Article 46. Nomination and Appointment of Officers

Article 47. Governor and Council Have Negative On Each Other

Article 48. Repealed

Article 49. President of Senate, Etc. to Act as Governor When Office Vacant; Speaker of House to Act When Office of President of Senate Also Vacant

Article 49-A. Prolonged Failure to Qualify; Vacancy in Office of Governor Due to Physical Or Mental Incapacity, Etc

Article 50. Governor to Prorogue Or Adjourn Legislature, and Call Extra Sessions

Article 51. Powers and Duties of Governor As Commander-in-Chief

Article 52. Pardoning Power

Article 53. Repealed

Article 54. Repealed

Article 55. Repealed

Article 56. Disbursements From Treasury

Article 57. Repealed

Article 58. Compensation of Governor and Council

Article 59. Salaries of Judges

COUNCIL – Page 50

Article 60. Councilors; Mode of Election, Etc

Article 61. Vacancies, How Filled, If No Choice

Article 62. Subsequent Vacancies; Governor to Convene; Duties

Article 63. Impeachment of Councilors

Article 64. Secretary to Record Proceedings of Council

Article 65. Councilor Districts Provided For

Article 66. Elections by Legislature May be Adjourned From Day to Day; Order Thereof

SECRETARY, TREASURER, ETC. – Page 53

Article 67. Election of Secretary and Treasurer

Article 68. State Records, Where Kept; Duty of Secretary

Article 69. Deputy Secretary

Article 70. Secretary to Give Bond

COUNTY TREASURER, ETC. – Page 54

Article 71. County Treasurers, Registers of Probate, County Attorneys, Sheriffs, and Registers of Deeds Elected

Article 72. Counties May be Divided Into Districts For Registering Deeds

JUDICIARY POWER – Page 55

Article 72-A. Supreme and Superior Courts

Article 73. Tenure of Office to be Expressed in Commissions; Judges to Hold Office During Good Behavior, Etc.; Removal

Article 73-A. Supreme Court, Administration

Article 74. Judges to Give Opinions, When

Article 75. Justices of Peace Commissioned For Five Years

Article 76. Divorce and Probate Appeals, Where Tried

Article 77. Jurisdiction of Justices in Civil Causes

Article 78. Judges and Sheriffs, When Disqualified by Age

Article 79. Judges and Justices not to Act As Counsel

Article 80. Jurisdiction and Term of Probate Courts

Article 81. Judges and Registers of Probate not to Act As Counsel

CLERKS OF COURTS – Page 58

Article 82. Clerks of Courts, by Whom Appointed

ENCOURAGEMENT OF LITERATURE, TRADE, ETC. – Page 59

Article 83. Encouragement of Literature, Etc.; Control of Corporations, Monopolies, Etc

OATHS AND SUBSCRIPTIONS EXCLUSION FROM OFFICES, ETC. – Page 61

Article 84. Oath of Civil Officers

Article 85. Before Whom Taken

Article 86. Form of Commissions

Article 87. Form of Writs

Article 88. Form of Indictments, Etc

Article 89. Suicides and Deodands

Article 90. Existing Laws Continued If not Repugnant

Article 91. Habeas Corpus

Article 92. Enacting Style of Statutes

Article 93. Governor and Judges Prohibited From Holding Other Offices

Article 94. Incompatibility of Offices; Only Two Offices of Profit to be Holden At Same Time

Article 95. Incompatibility of Certain Offices

Article 96. Bribery and Corruption Disqualify For Office

Article 97. Repealed

Article 98. Constitution, When to Take Effect

Article 99. Repealed

Article 100. Alternate Methods of Proposing Amendments

Article 101. Enrollment of Constitution

The Constitution of The State of Rhode Island

Preamble – Page 21

Article I: Declaration of Certain Constitutional Rights and Principles – Page 22

Section 1. Right to Make and Alter Constitution - Constitution Obligatory Upon All

Section 2. Laws for Good of Whole - Burdens to be Equally Distributed - Due Process - Equal Protection - Discrimination - No Right to Abortion Granted

Section 3. Freedom of Religion

Section 4. Slavery Prohibited - Slavery Shall not be Permitted in this State

Section 5. Entitlement to Remedies for Injuries and Wrongs - Right to Justice

Section 6. Search and Seizure

Section 7. Requirement of Presentment or Indictment - Information by Attorney-General - Grand Juries - Double Jeopardy

Section 8. Bail, Fines and Punishments

Section 9. Right to bail - Habeas Corpus

Section 10. Rights of Accused Persons in Criminal Proceedings

Section 11. Relief of Debtors from Prison

Section 12. Ex Post Facto Laws - Laws Impairing Obligation of Contract

Section 13. Self-Crimination

Section 14. Presumption Of Innocence - Securing Accused Persons

Section 15. Trial by Jury

Section 16. Compensation for Taking of Private Property for Public Use - Regulation of Fishery Rights and Shore Privileges Not Public Taking

Section 17. Fishery Rights - Shore Privileges - Preservation of Natural Resources

Section 18. Subordination of Military to Civil Authority - Martial Law

Section 19. Quartering of soldiers

Section 20. Freedom of Press

Section 21. Right to Assembly - Redress of Grievances - Freedom of Speech

Section 22. Right to Bear Arms

Section 23. Rights of Victims of Crime

Section 24. Rights not Enumerated - State Rights not Dependent on Federal Rights

Article II: Suffrage – Page 29

Section 1. Persons Entitled to Vote

Section 2. Nomination of Candidates — Voter Registration — Absentee Voting — Conduct of Elections — Residency

Article III: Qualification for Office – Page 30

Section 1. Qualified Electors

Section 2. Disqualification Upon Conviction or Plea Of Nolo Contendere — Re-Qualification Following Sentence, Probation or Parole

Section 3. Oath of General Officers

Section 4. Oath of General Assembly Members, Judges, and Other Officers

Section 5. Administration of Oaths.

Section 6. Holding of Offices Under Other Governments – Senators and Representatives not to Hold Other Appointed Offices Under State Government

Section 7. Ethical Conduct.

Section 8. Ethics Commission — Code of Ethics

Article IV: Elections and Campaign Finance – Page 33

Section 1. Election and Terms of Governor, Lieutenant Governor, Secretary of State, Attorney-General, General Treasurer, and General Assembly Members

Section 2. Election by Plurality

Section 3. Filling Vacancy Caused by Death, Removal, Refusal to Serve, or Incapacity of Elected Officers -- Election when no Candidate Receives Plurality

Section 4. Temporary Appointment to Fill Vacancies in Office of Secretary of State, Attorney-General, or General Treasurer

Section 5. Special Elections to Fill General Assembly Vacancies

Section 6. Elections in Grand Committee – Majority Vote – Term Of Elected Official

Section 7. Elections in Grand Committee – Quorum – Permitted Activities

Section 8. Voter Registration Lists

Section 9. Reports of Campaign Contributions and Expenses

Section 10. Limitations on Campaign Contributions – Public Financing of Campaign Expenditures of General Officers

Article V: Distribution of Powers – Page 38

Section 1. Distribution of Powers

Article VI: Legislative Power – Page 39

Section 1. Constitution Supreme Law of the State

Section 2. Power Vested in General Assembly – Concurrence of Houses Required to Enact Laws – Style of Laws

Section 3. Sessions of General Assembly – Compensation of General Assembly Members and Officers

Section 4. Restriction on General Assembly Members Activities as Counsel

Section 5. Immunities of General Assembly Members

Section 6. Election and Qualification of General Assembly Members – Quorum and Organization of Houses

Section 7. Rules of houses – Contempt

Section 8. House Journals

Section 9. Adjournment of Houses

Section 10. Continuation of Previous Powers

Section 11. Vote Required to Pass Local or Private Appropriations

Section 12. Property Valuations for Tax Assessments

Section 13. Continuance in Office Until Successors Qualify

Section 14. General Corporation Laws

Section 15. Lotteries

Section 16. Borrowing Power of General Assembly

Section 17. Borrowing in Anticipation of Receipts

Section 18. Redevelopment Powers

Section 19. Taking of Property for Highways, Streets, Places, Parks or Parkways

Section 20. Local Off-Street Parking Facilities

Section 21. Emergency Powers in Case of Enemy Attack

Section 22. Restriction of Gambling

Article VII: House of Representatives – Page 47

Section 1. Composition

Section 2. Officers

Article VIII: Senate – Page 48

Section 1. Composition

Section 2. Lieutenant Governor to be Presiding Officer until 2003

Section 3. Repealed

Section 4. Repealed

Article IX: Executive Power – Page 49

Section 1. Power Vested in Governor

Section 2. Faithful Execution of Laws

Section 3. Captain General and Commander in Chief of Military and Navy

Section 4. Reprieves

Section 5. Powers of Appointment

Section 6. Adjournment of General Assembly

Section 7. Convening of Special Sessions of the General Assembly

Section 8. Commissions

Section 9. Vacancy in Office of Governor

Section 10. Vacancies in Both Offices of Governor and Lieutenant Governor

Section 11. Compensation of Governor and Lieutenant Governor

Section 12. Powers and Duties of Secretary, Attorney-General, and General Treasurer

Section 13. Pardons

Section 14. Veto Power of Governor

Section 15. State Budget

Section 16. Limitation on State Spending. [Effective July 1, 2007 until July 1, 2012]

Section 16. Limitation on State Spending

Section 17. Budget Reserve Account

Article X: Judicial Power – Page 56

Section 1. Power Vested in Court

Section 2. Jurisdiction of Supreme and Inferior Courts

Section 3. Advisory Opinions By Supreme Court

Section 4. State Court Judges – Judicial Selection

Section 5. Tenure of Supreme Court Justices

Section 6. Judges of Supreme Court – Compensation

Section 7. Wardens and Justices of the Peace

Article XI: Impeachments – Page 58

Section 1. Power to Impeach – Procedure

Section 2. Trial of Impeachments

Section 3. Officers Subject to Impeachment -- Grounds and Effect of Conviction

Article XII: Education – Page 60

Section 1. Duty of General Assembly to Promote Schools and Libraries

Section 2. Perpetual School Fund

Section 3. Donations

Section 4. Implementation of Article

Article XIII: Home Rule for Cities and Towns – Page 61

Section 1. Intent of Article

Section 2. Local Legislative Powers

Section 3. Local Legislative Bodies

Section 4. Powers of General Assembly Over Cities and Towns

Section 5. Local Taxing and Borrowing Powers

Section 6. Charter Commissions

Section 7. Adoption of Charters

Section 8. Amendments to Charters

Section 9. Filing of Charter Petitions to Bicameral Legislative Bodies

Section 10. Charter certificates – Signing – Recordation – Deposit – Judicial notice

Section 11. Judicial Powers Unaffected by Article

Article XIV: Constitutional Amendments and Revision – Page 65

Section 1. Procedure for Proposing and Approving Amendments

Section 2. Constitutional Conventions

Article XV: General Transition – Page 66

Section 1. Rights and Duties of Public Bodies Unaffected – Continuation of Laws, Ordinances, Regulations and Rules

Section 2. Validity of Bonds, Debts, Contracts, Suits, Actions, and Rights of Actions Continued

Section 3. Continuation of Office Holders

Section 4. Implementing Legislation for Article III, Sections 7 and 8, and Article IV, section 10

The Constitution of the
State of Vermont:

CHAPTER I: A DECLARATION OF THE RIGHTS OF THE INHABITANTSOF THE STATE OF VERMONT – Page 16

Article 1. All Persons Born Free; Their Natural Rights; Slavery Prohibited

Article 2. Private Property Subject to Public Use; Owner to be Paid

Article 3. Freedom in Religion; Right and Duty of Religious Worship

Article 4. Remedy at Law Secured to All

Article 5. Internal Police

Article 6. Officers Servants of the People

Article 7. Government for the People; They May Change It

Article 8. Elections to be Free and Pure; Rights of Voters Therein

Article 9. Citizens Rights and Duties in the State; Bearing Arms; Taxation

Article 10. Rights of Persons Accused of Crime; Personal Liberty; Waiver o f Jury Trial

Article 11. Search and Seizure Regulated

Article 12. Trial by Jury to be Held Sacred

Article 13. Freedom of Speech and of the Press

Article 14. Immunity for Words Spoken in Legislative Debate

Article 15. Legislature Only May Suspend Laws

Article 16. Right to Bear Arms; Standing Armies; Military Power Subordinate to Civil

Article 17. Martial Law Restricted

Article 18. Regard to Fundamental Principles and Virtues Necessary to Preserve Liberty

Article 19. Right to Emigrate

Article 20. Right to Assemble, Instruct and Petition

Article 21. No Transportation for Trial

CHAPTER II: PLAN OR FRAME OF GOVERNMENT

DELEGATION AND DISTRIBUTION OF POWERS – Page 22

Article 1. Governing Power

Article 2. Supreme Legislative Power

Article 3. Supreme Executive Power

Article 4. Judiciary

Article 5. Departments to be Distinct

Legislative Department – Page 23

Article 6. Legislative Powers

Article 7. Biennial Sessions

Article 8. Doors of General Assembly to be Open

Article 9. Journals; Yeas and Nays

Article 10. Style of Laws

Article 11. Governor to Approve Bills; Veto Proceedings Thereon; Non-action

Article 12. Fees for Advocating Bills, Etc.

Article 13. Representatives; Number

Article 14. Powers of House

Article 15. Residence of Representatives and Senators

Article 16. Representatives Oaths

Article 17. Oath of Senators and Representatives

Article 18. Senators; Numbers; Qualifications

Article 19. Powers of Senate; Lieutenant-Governor's Duties

EXECUTIVE DEPARTMENT – Page 29

Article 20. Governor; Executive Power

Article 21. Secretary of Civil and Military Affairs

Article 22. Commissions; State Seal

Article 23. Residence Of Governor And Lieutenant-Governor

Article 24. Vacancy in Office of Governor, Lieutenant-Governor and Treasurer

Article 25. Security Given by Treasurer and Sheriffs

Article 26. Treasurer's Accounts

Article 27. Drawing Money From Treasury

JUDICIARY DEPARTMENT – Page 32

Article 28. Courts of Justice

Article 29. The Supreme Court; Composition

Article 30. Supreme Court; Jurisdiction

Article 31. Lower Courts; Jurisdiction

Article 32. Filling Judicial Vacancies

Article 33. Interim Judicial Appointments

Article 34. Judicial Term of Office

Article 35. Mandatory Retirement

Article 36. Suspension and Removal; Implementation Procedures for Sections 32 Through 36

Article 37. Rule-Making Power

Article 38. Jury Trials

Article 39. Forms of Prosecutions and Indictments; Fines

Article 40. Excessive Bail Prohibited; Prisoners Bailable; Imprisonment for Debt Prohibited

Article 41. Habeas Corpus

**QUALIFICATIONS OF FREEMEN
AND FREEWOMEN** – Page 37

Article 42. Voter's Qualifications and Oath

ELECTIONS; OFFICERS; TERMS OF OFFICE – Page 38

Article 43. Biennial Elections

Article 44. Election of Representatives and Senators

Article 45. Manner of Election

Article 46. Terms of Senators and Representatives

Article 47. Election of Governor, Lieutenant-Governor and Treasurer

Article 48. Election of Secretary of State and Auditor of Accounts

Article 49. Term of Governor, Lieutenant-Governor and Treasurer

Article 50. Election of Assistant Judges, Sheriffs and State's Attorneys

Article 51. Election of Judges of Probate

Article 52. Election of Justices of the Peace; Apportionment

Article 53. Election of Assistant Judges, Sheriffs, State's Attorneys, Judges of Probate, and Justices of the Peace

Article 54. Incompatible Offices

Article 55. Freedom of Elections; Bribery

OATH OF ALLEGIANCE; OATH OF OFFICE – Page 42

Article 56. Oaths of Allegiance and Office

IMPEACHMENT – Page 43

Article 57. Impeachments, House May Order

Article 58. Liability To; Senate To Try; Judgment

MILITIA – Page 44

Article 59. Militia

GENERAL PROVISIONS – Page 45

Article 60. Legislature Restricted

Article 61. Offices of Profit; Compensation; Illegal Fees

Article 62. Record of Deeds

Article 64. Punishment at Hard Labor, When

Article 65. Suicide's Estate not Forfeited; No Deodand

Article 66. Citizenship

Article 67. Hunting; Fowling and Fishing

Article 68. Laws to Encourage Virtue and Prevent Vice; Schools; Religious Activities

Article 69. Charters, Limit on Right to Grant

Article 70. Workers Compensation

Article 71. Declaration of Rights not to be Violated

AMENDMENT OF THE CONSTITUTION – Page 49

Article 72. Amending Constitution

Article 73. Manner of Apportionment of the General Assembly

TEMPORARY PROVISIONS – Page 51

Article 74. Extension of Terms of Certain Officers

Article 75. Revision of Chapter II

Article 76. Inclusive Language Revision

www.ingramcontent.com/pod-product-compliance
Lightning Source LLC
Chambersburg PA
CBHW071425220526
45469CB00004B/1433